The Edwards family

SOUTH AFRICA

landscapes

SOUTH AFRICA
landscapes

Struik Publishers (a division of New Holland Publishing (South Africa) (Pty) Ltd)
80 McKenzie Street, Cape Town 8001
www.struik.co.za
New Holland Publishing is a member of the Johnnic Publishing Group

Log on to our photographic website www.imagesofafrica.co.za for an African experience.

First published 1997

7 9 10 8 6

Designer: Laurence Lemmon-Warde
Captions: Anouska Good
Cover design: Janice Evans and Laurence Lemmon-Warde
Cartographer: Desireé Oosterberg
Managing editor: Annlerie van Rooyen
Proofreader: Glynne Newlands
Reproduction: Hirt & Carter Cape (Pty) Ltd
Printed and bound in Hong Kong by Sing Cheong Printing Company Limited

ISBN 1 86872 014 4

FRONT COVER A small fishing boat awaits high tide at Muizenberg beach, Cape Town.
SPINE Springbok quench their thirst in the arid Kgalagadi Transfrontier Park.
BACK COVER Spring brings on a riotous display of colour, carpeting the Namaqualand landscape.
HALF TITLE Goegap Nature Reserve near Springbok lies at the heart of the springtime wildflower region.
TITLE Near Montagu, on the edge of the Little Karoo, isolated cottages dot the landscape.
THESE PAGES The sun sets over the Lower Sabie River in the Kruger National Park.
FOLLOWING PAGE The beautiful eastern Free State is home to the Basotho people.

PHOTOGRAPHIC CREDITS

Contents

ZIMBABWE

BOTSWANA

Musina

Great Limpopo Transfrontier Park

LIMPOPO PROVINCE

○ Tzaneen

POLOKWANE ●

Kruger National Park

Blyde River Canyon Nature Reserve

Pilgrim's Rest ○

⌂ Skukuza

Limpopo

Kgalagadi Transfrontier Park

Pilanesberg National Park

Mmabatho ●

PRETORIA ●

Nelspruit ○

MOZAMBIQUE

● **MAPUTO**

NORTH-WEST

JOHANNESBURG ● ● **MPUMALANGA**

Soweto ○

GAUTENG

SWAZILAND

Molopo

Kroonstad ●

Vaal

Itala Game Reserve ● ● Mkuzi Game Reserve

Kosi Bay

Upington ●

Augrabies Falls National Park

Richtersveld National Park

NAMIBIA

Gariep (Orange)

FREE STATE

Golden Gate Highlands National Park

Hluhluwe-Umfolozi Park

Sodwana Bay

KIMBERLEY ●

BLOEMFONTEIN ●

KWAZULU-NATAL

Greater St Lucia Wetland Park

Tugela

ATLANTIC OCEAN

Springbok ○

NORTHERN CAPE

Gariep (Orange)

LESOTHO

Royal Natal National Park

MALUTI

Umzimkulu

● **PIETERMARITZBURG**

● **DURBAN**

Namaqualand

SOUTH AFRICA

DRAKENSBERG

N

St Helena Bay

Olifants

CEDARBERG

Karoo National Park

EASTERN CAPE

Port St Johns ○

Paternoster ○

Lamberts Bay ○

HEXRIVIERBERGE

Beaufort West ●

Graaff-Reinet ●

Umtata ●

Great Kei

Saldanha Bay

West Coast National Park

Paarl ●

Montagu ●

Klein-Karoo

Oudtshoorn ●

Nature's Valley

Addo Elephant National Park

Great Fish

Grahamstown ○

● **EAST LONDON**

CAPE TOWN ●

Franschhoek ○

Stellenbosch ○

Caledon ○

WESTERN CAPE

George ● Knysna ●

Sundays

OUTENIQUA

Wilderness National Park

Tsitsikamma National Park

Plettenberg Bay

● **PORT ELIZABETH**

Cape Point

Hermanus ○

False Bay

Waenhuiskrans ●

Cape Agulhas

INDIAN OCEAN

AFRICA

PREVIOUS PAGES Table Mountain, flanked by Devil's Peak on the left and Lion's Head and Signal Hill on the right, forms an impressive backdrop to Cape Town.

LEFT Reaching above the clouds, Lion's Head offers incomparable views of the city and ocean. A relatively easy trail leads to its summit.

ABOVE The colourful coons are a feature of the city and take to the streets during the New Year celebrations.

FOLLOWING PAGES The bustling Victoria and Alfred Waterfront complex is the city's most successful tourist venture, offering shops, restaurants, pubs, an aquarium and cinemas, to name but a few attractions.

PREVIOUS PAGES Situated on the Atlantic seaboard, Clifton's famous Fourth Beach is a favourite haunt of Cape Town's sun-worshippers.

ABOVE Chapman's Peak Drive, between Hout Bay and Noordhoek, is undoubtedly among the world's most breathtaking scenic drives. It is closed periodically owing to rock falls.

RIGHT Hout Bay is the site of a thriving fishing industry. Part of the harbour has been converted into a marine emporium known as Mariner's Wharf.

FOLLOWING PAGES The inviting waters of False Bay lap the east coast of the Cape Peninsula. A string of towns and villages, many of them popular holiday resorts, lines its shores.

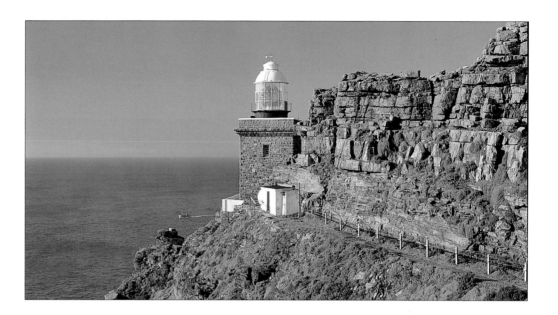

LEFT AND TOP Sheer cliffs plunge into the often turbulent seas at Cape Point. The lighthouse, situated close to the water's edge, warns of the dangers of this treacherous stretch of coastline.

ABOVE Baboons roam the surrounding Cape of Good Hope Nature Reserve.

ABOVE AND RIGHT The Kirstenbosch National Botanical Garden was created on land once owned by mining magnate Cecil John Rhodes. Covering 560 hectares, the gardens support a rich diversity of plant species and birdlife.

PREVIOUS PAGES The luxurious Grande Roche Hotel is set in the Paarl winelands and offers gracious accommodation and outstanding cuisine.

LEFT Nestling in the shelter of the Jonkershoek Mountains, historic Lanzerac near Stellenbosch is an example of classic Cape Dutch architecture.

BELOW Although Stellenbosch may be better known as a wine region, it also has delicious strawberries on offer.

ABOVE Established by the Huguenots in 1688, picturesque Franschhoek remains true to its French origins and is renowned for its many fine restaurants and excellent wines. Despite this the town has managed to retain its rural charm.

RIGHT The twists and turns of the Franschhoek Pass provide superb views over the lush Berg River valley. In winter, the road may be blocked by snowfalls.

OPPOSITE The fertile Hex River Valley is the source of most of South Africa's export grapes. Seasons are marked by the colours of the vines, which change from vibrant summer green to russet autumnal shades.

ABOVE Passengers on the Blue Train can enjoy the superb spectacle of the Hex River Mountains and valley.

RIGHT The agricultural wealth of the region supports around 200 farms, all dedicated to the cultivation of the grape.

FOLLOWING PAGES The long expanse of beach at the Strand is one of South Africa's safest and is popular with both swimming and boating enthusiasts.

LEFT Chiselled by wind and water, the Wolfberg Arch is just one of the Cedarberg's dramatic sandstone formations.

ABOVE Reminders of the San people, the original inhabitants of the Cedarberg, remain in their rock paintings.

ABOVE Colourful boats lie in readiness at Paternoster, one of the West Coast's most attractive fishing villages.

RIGHT This quaint cottage at St Helena Bay gives no indication of the area's status as the commercial fishing centre of South Africa.

BELOW Benefitting from the huge shoals of pilchards and anchovies, large colonies of Cape gannets congregate along the West Coast.

PREVIOUS PAGES Every year, after the winter rains, the otherwise harsh Namaqualand landscape is transformed into a vibrant carpet of wildflowers. The seeds of these hardy plants are drought-resistant and lie dormant throughout the dry months.

LEFT Gemsbok graze in the Kgalagadi Transfrontier Park, which includes the former Kalahari Gemsbok National Park, founded in 1931 to protect the rapidly dwindling herds of both gemsbok and springbok.

ABOVE The Augrabies Falls are some of the largest in the world and are formed from 19 separate waterfalls which plummet 56 metres to the pool below.

ABOVE *Kokerbome*, or quiver trees (*Aloe dichotoma*), are characteristic of the dramatic Richtersveld. The local Khoikhoi people used the bark of this plant to make arrow quivers.

LEFT Although much of the Richtersveld is a national park, the indigenous Nama people retain ownership of the land and continue to farm livestock.

RIGHT *Halfmens*, or elephant's trunk, trees are just one of the botanical riches present within the park. These plants always face north in order to maximize photosynthesis.

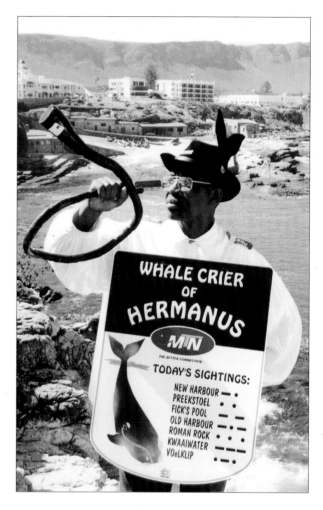

ABOVE The whale crier of Hermanus signals the presence of southern right whales in Walker Bay. The town has built up a considerable tourist industry around these whales which come to mate and calve along this stretch of coast from July to November.

FOLLOWING PAGES Golden wheat fields stretch across the countryside in the Caledon district. Although an agricultural centre, the area is better known for its famous hot springs and annual Wild Flower Show.

OPPOSITE Waenhuiskrans, also known as Arniston, is a charming fishing village which has retained a 19th-century atmosphere. Its two names are taken from a British vessel, the *Arniston*, wrecked in 1815, and a nearby sea cavern known as Waenhuiskrans, or 'wagon house cliff'.

ABOVE The lighthouse at Cape Agulhas, the southernmost point on the African continent, was built in 1848 and is now a museum.

PREVIOUS PAGES The rolling hills and rich green pastures of the Overberg region are perfect for sheep farming.

ABOVE A small cove tucked between steep cliffs, Victoria Bay is internationally renowned for its surfing. A cluster of holiday homes lines the beach.

RIGHT The Outeniqua Choo-Tjoe runs between George and Knysna, crossing the Kaaimans River bridge en route. The journey takes just over three hours and passes through some of the Garden Route's most beautiful scenery.

FOLLOWING PAGES The charming coastal resort of Wilderness lies to the west of Knysna, at the mouth of the Touws River.

PREVIOUS PAGES Apart from being the source of Knysna's famous oysters, Knysna Lagoon is home to over 200 species of fish as well as crabs and prawns.

LEFT Plettenberg Bay is one of South Africa's most fashionable holiday destinations with safe, wide-open beaches and numerous hotels, including Beacon Island.

BELOW The beautiful and much sought after 'pansy shell' is the symbol of Plettenberg Bay.

BOTTOM Nature's Valley is a small village and reserve at the bottom of the Groot River Pass.

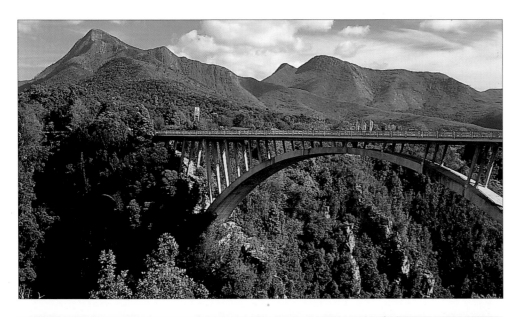

TOP The spectacular Paul Sauer Bridge spans the Storms River.

ABOVE The Knysna loerie is often seen in the Garden Route's forests.

RIGHT Several trails meander through the indigenous Knysna Forest.

LEFT Created by erosion, the Valley of Desolation near Graaff-Reinet, with its bizarre dolerite peaks and pillars, has been proclaimed a national monument.

ABOVE The Little Karoo is famous for its ostriches with Oudtshoorn once considered to be the 'feather capital' of the world.

FOLLOWING PAGES The Karoo covers a vast region; the main motorway passes through a seemingly endless and unchanging landscape.

LEFT Port Elizabeth's Oceanarium is well known for its dolphins and their spectacular displays.

ABOVE Situated northeast of the city, the Addo Elephant National Park was established in 1931 to preserve the highly endangered Cape elephant. Buffalo and rhino also inhabit the park.

RIGHT The beaches at Port Elizabeth cater to all tastes, offering sailing, rubber-ducking, surfing and beach sports.

ABOVE A Xhosa boy plays a home-made guitar. Although traditional customs are still upheld, western influences are apparent.

RIGHT The hilly Katberg region with its crisp inland climate is popular with both hikers and horseriders.

LEFT The sun rises over East London's Eastern Beach, a popular surfing spot.

ABOVE At the spectacular detached cliff known as the Hole-in-the-Wall, surf thunders through an archway giving rise to the local Xhosa name of *esiKhaleni*, 'place of the noise'.

FOLLOWING PAGES The Eastern Cape, including the former Ciskei and Transkei regions, is the home of the Xhosa. Traditional huts lie scattered across the hills.

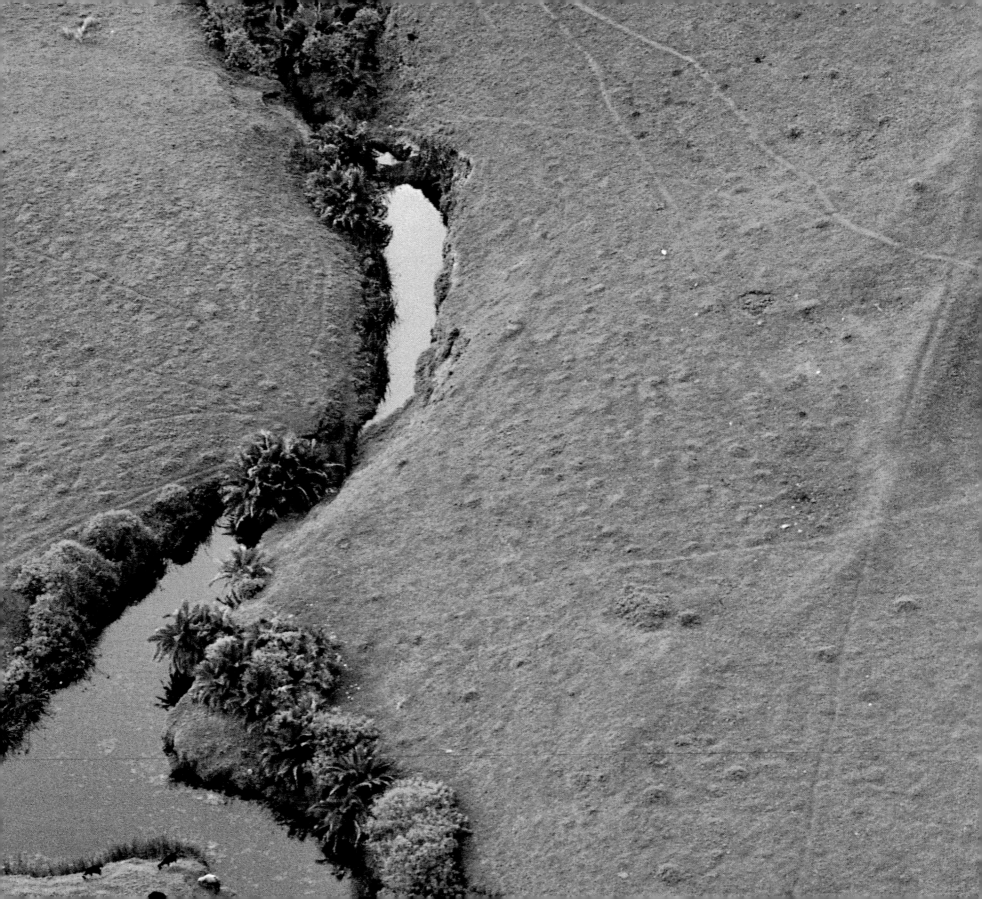

ABOVE Elaborately attired ricksha drivers seek out customers on Durban's beachfront, a 6-kilometre stretch known as the Golden Mile.

RIGHT Durban's City Hall was built in 1910 and is an almost exact replica of the city hall in Belfast, Northern Ireland.

FOLLOWING PAGES Fishermen haul in their nets while, across the water, an imposing line of upmarket hotels extends the length of the Golden Mile.

OPPOSITE Picturesque Howick Falls is a popular photographic subject for tourists.
The falls drop 95 metres into the Umgeni River.

ABOVE The charming Victorian bandstand is just one of the attractions in Pietermaritzburg's
Alexandra Park. An art exhibition is held in the park each May.

FOLLOWING PAGES Shaka's Rock on the KwaZulu-Natal north coast offers shark-protected
swimming and pleasant picnic facilities.

PREVIOUS PAGES The Drakensberg, hewn into deep gorges and ridges, is South Africa's highest mountain range.

LEFT A floral and wildlife sanctuary, the Royal Natal National Park is known for its scenic beauty.

ABOVE Giant's Castle is a hiker's paradise with over 800 species of flowering plants and numerous birds of prey.

FOLLOWING PAGES The impressive 500-metre-high wall of the Amphitheatre stretches across 5 kilometres and forms part of the Mont-aux-Sources massif.

PREVIOUS PAGES Renowned for its rhino conservation programme, the Hluhluwe-Umfolozi Park sustains populations of both black and white rhino.

LEFT Located in the extreme north of KwaZulu-Natal, Itala Game Reserve is home to the province's only population of tsessebe.

ABOVE Traditional Zulu dancers perform at Shakaland, a complex dedicated to exploring all aspects of the Zulu culture, from hut-building to herbal remedies.

PREVIOUS PAGES At Cape Vidal the barrier dunes characteristic of the Maputaland coastline change to form a low-lying expanse of gently undulating dunes.

ABOVE Kudus are among the many species of buck that can be found in the Mkuzi Game Reserve; others include eland, nyala, duiker and reedbuck.

RIGHT The Greater St Lucia area is known for its forests of wild figs. These are especially plentiful along the banks of the Pongolo River.

FOLLOWING PAGES Kosi Bay, despite its name, is not a bay but an estuary located at the end of a chain of four interconnecting lakes.

LEFT Vast fields of sunflowers, one of the principal crops of the Free State, can be seen throughout the province.

ABOVE The Basotho people are known for their distinctive hats and colourful, beautifully patterned blankets, both of which form part of their national costume.

FOLLOWING PAGES Snow covers the land in the Free State's Golden Gate Highlands National Park, an area of subtly hued, sculpted sandstone formations.

ABOVE Waterfalls are a feature of the Escarpment. The Berlin Falls tumble 80 metres over lichen-encrusted rock into the pool below.

RIGHT Scenic Long Tom Pass is named after the huge Creusot artillery gun used against the British during the Anglo-Boer War (1899-1902).

LEFT The Blydepoort Dam is just one of the scenic highlights along the course of the Blyde River.

ABOVE Once a prosperous 19th-century gold-mining town, Pilgrim's Rest is today preserved as a living museum.

ABOVE Bourke's Luck Potholes have been scoured out of yellow dolerite by the swirling waters at the confluence of the Treur and Blyde rivers.

RIGHT The Three Rondavels massif overlooks the majestic Blyde River Canyon, considered to be one of southern Africa's greatest natural wonders.

PREVIOUS PAGES The Kruger National Park has been combined with Limpopo and Gonarezhou national parks in Mozambique and Zimbabwe to form the Great Limpopo Transfrontier Park.

TOP AND ABOVE Buffalo roam the Kruger in huge herds. The park is also home to many bird species, including bateleur eagles.

RIGHT Perched on a cliff, Olifants Camp offers spectacular views over the Olifants River.

LEFT Although there are almost 1 000 leopards in the Kruger National Park, they are seldom seen during daylight hours as they are nocturnal hunters.

ABOVE A pair of giraffe survey the surrounding landscape.

OPPOSITE A baobab tree stands silhouetted against the evening sky near Skukuza, the Kruger Park's headquarters.

RIGHT The largest of Africa's carnivores, the 'King of the Beasts' possesses phenomenal strength and knows no natural enemies.

BELOW Sabi Sabi is a privately owned game reserve renowned as much for its luxurious facilities as for its game-viewing.

LEFT The road to Pretoriuskop, the Kruger National Park's oldest camp, meanders across a gently rolling plain.

ABOVE Approximately 8 000 elephants inhabit the park.

FOLLOWING PAGES The land around Tzaneen is given over to the production of tea, the basis of the region's agricultural economy.

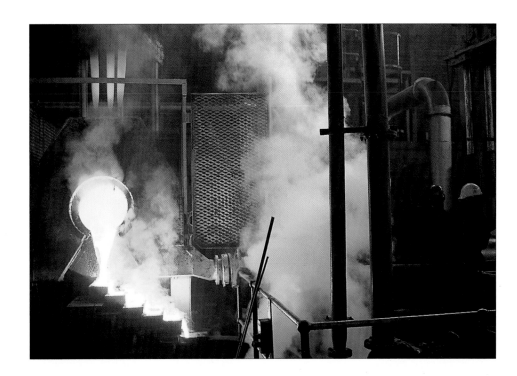

LEFT The country's largest metropolis, Johannesburg, is a vibrant, modern, yet uniquely African city.

ABOVE Gold is the foundation stone on which Johannesburg, South Africa's business capital, was built.

ABOVE Located on the site of an old mine, Gold Reef City recreates Johannesburg's pioneer days. Attractions include traditional dancing, period-style shops and a tour of a mine shaft.

RIGHT Diagonal Street, lined with soaring glass skyscrapers, is at the heart of Johannesburg's bustling Newtown district.

ABOVE Over 70 000 lilac-blossomed jacarandas have been planted in Pretoria's parks, gardens and along its streets, giving rise to its name of 'Jacaranda City'.

RIGHT Designed by Sir Herbert Baker, the magnificent neo-classical Union Buildings look out over Pretoria. They are the national government's administrative headquarters.

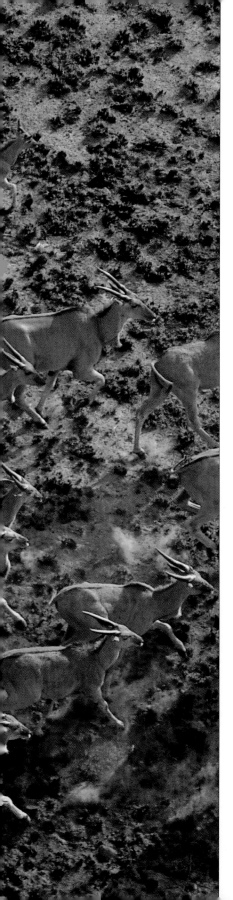

LEFT Eland, originally brought in from Namibia as part of a game-stocking programme, now flourish in the Pilanesberg National Park.

ABOVE An early morning hot-air balloon ride over the Pilanesberg National Park enables visitors to enjoy game-viewing with a difference.

FOLLOWING PAGES The Palace, the centrepiece of Sun City's Lost City development, is a fantasy hotel complete with domes, minarets, and a man-made jungle in the grounds.

ABOVE Artificially generated waves contribute to the illusion of a tropical beach paradise at Sun City's Valley of Waves. Waterskiing, windsurfing and parasailing are available at the nearby Waterworld.